Janice Hanna

EVERYDAY

Love

Spiritual Refreshment
for Women

BARBOUR
PUBLISHING

Cover design: Kirk DouPonce, DogEared Design

Published by Barbour Publishing, Inc., P.O. Box 719, Uhrichsville, Ohio 44683
www.barbourbooks.com

Our mission is to publish and distribute inspirational products offering exceptional value and biblical encouragement to the masses.

Member of the
Evangelical Christian
Publishers Association

Printed in India.

Contents

Introduction

When you hear the words *everyday love*, what comes to mind? A comfortable day-in and day-out love for spouse and family? A walking, talking love relationship with the Creator of the universe? The ability to love coworkers and friends in spite of their flaws? *Love* is one of those words that we use all the time—and often out of context. We say, "I love this pizza!" or "I love that TV show!" But when it comes to loving people, well, that's sometimes a bit harder. It's tough to love others when they're not treating us as they should. And it's even harder when the wounds run deep. But God shows us, through His Word, how to love even the most unlovable person. And He reveals His great love for us within the pages of that great book as well. Let's journey together down the road toward everyday love.

Deep and Wide

No Boundaries!

For as high as the heavens are above the earth, so great is his love for those who fear him; as far as the east is from the west, so far has he removed our transgressions from us.

PSALM 103:11–12 NIV

God's love for us surpasses all boundaries. If we go to the highest highs or the lowest lows, He will meet us there. No matter where we are in our faith journey, He stands with arms wide, ready to forgive our sins. We don't understand this kind of love. Then again, if we could understand it, perhaps it wouldn't feel like such a gift. Thank God for a love that knows no boundaries.

Too Wonderful
to Be Measured

*I want you to know all about
Christ's love, although it is too wonderful
to be measured. Then your lives
will be filled with all that God is.*

EPHESIANS 3:19 CEV

Have you ever thought about measuring
God's love? There's no ruler long enough!
No map wide enough. No ocean deep
enough. God's love is immeasurable. It is,
as we sang as children, deep and wide. If we
spent our lives trying to make sense of
it, it would only outrun us in the end.

A Love That Reaches
to the Heavens

Your love, LORD, reaches to the
heavens, your faithfulness to the skies.

PSALM 36:5 NIV

Isn't it interesting to picture God's love
sweeping over all of humanity? From
His throne in heaven, He pours out this
marvelous fountain of love. And with His
arms spread wide on the cross, it flowed as
a sacrifice for all. His love reaches us when
we're in the low places and chases after us
when we're in seasons of rebellion. Praise
God for His sweeping love!

Nothing Can Separate Us

*For I am convinced that neither
death nor life, neither angels nor
demons, neither the present nor the
future, nor any powers, neither height
nor depth, nor anything else in all
creation, will be able to separate
us from the love of God that is
in Christ Jesus our Lord.*

ROMANS 8:38–39 NIV

Have you ever felt as if you're unlovable?
Here's some great news: nothing you've
ever done—no sin you've committed, no
wicked thought that's flitted through your
brain, no temptation you've fallen into—can
separate you from God's love. Even when
you feel far removed from Him, He's still
there, extending His arms of love.

Unconditional Love

Come live in my heart and pay no rent.

SAMUEL LOVER

Unconditional love doesn't say, "I'll love you *if.*" No, real love doesn't charge rent. It's a gift, one we freely receive and freely offer to others. Today as you consider God's unconditional love for you, why not thank Him that the only cost was the one He paid through the death of His Son on the cross for your sins.

The Greatest Gift

For God So Loved...

*For God so loved the world, that he gave
his only begotten Son, that whosoever
believeth in him should not perish,
but have everlasting life.*

JOHN 3:16 KJV

If we spent the rest of our lives trying to
figure out the heart of God for His people,
we couldn't do it. What kind of father
gives his son as a sacrifice for the lives of
countless billions of people? And all He asks
in response is that we believe so that we can
receive His immeasurable gift of love. Today
open your heart to believe and receive!

Laying Down Your Life

"Greater love has no one than this:
to lay down one's life for one's friends."

JOHN 15:13 NIV

Have you ever wondered if you would be willing—or able—to lay down your life for someone else (say, a family member, child, or spouse)? Could you do it? Very few human beings have literally laid down their lives. However, Jesus, who lived a sinless life, willingly gave Himself as a sacrifice for us, His friends. He laid down His life so that we can have life eternal. Oh, what love!

This Is What Love Is. . .

This is how we know what love is:
Jesus Christ laid down his life for us.
And we ought to lay down our
lives for our brothers and sisters.

1 JOHN 3:16 NIV

Do you want to know what love is? It's the ability to sacrifice—to lay down personal wants and wishes—for others. Jesus gave us the ultimate example of sacrificial love when He walked up Calvary's hill and took our place on the cross. When we let go of selfishness and pride and put others first, we're following His lead. What an awesome display of love!

His Great Love

*But God showed his great love for us
by sending Christ to die for us
while we were still sinners.*

ROMANS 5:8 NLT

Have you ever tried to think up ways to
show others that you love them? Maybe you
send roses or write a great letter. Perhaps
you go out of your way to do something
sacrificial so that they will recognize your
great love. God went out of His way to show
us how much He loves us by offering His
only Son. What an amazing example of how
to love!

The Gift of Love

Love is, above all, the gift of oneself.

JEAN ANOUILH

Wondering what gift you can give the ones you love? Why not the gift of you? The people in your life need your time, your energy, your attention, and your love. They desire your encouragement, your energy, and your uplifting smile. All of the best presents you could offer would never come close to the one they most desire—you!

Love's Fruit

A Fruit Tree

But the fruit of the Spirit is love, joy, peace, forbearance, kindness, goodness, faithfulness, gentleness and self-control. Against such things there is no law.

GALATIANS 5:22–23 NIV

If love were a tree, it would be heavy with fruit. What fruit, you ask? Oh, many varieties! When you love people, you're naturally more patient with them. And you treat them kindly and use self-control. You're faithful to those you love, and you respond in a gentle fashion. These things are the "fruit" of a love relationship that comes from on high.

The Power of Life
and Death

*The tongue has the power of life
and death, and those who love it
will eat its fruit.*

PROVERBS 18:21 NIV

Have you ever been around people who
have sharp tongues? They don't come
across as loving, do they? No, they convey
just the opposite. The Bible tells us that
the power of life and death is found in the
tongue. When we speak words of love, we
bring life. When we offer sharp retorts and
ugly criticism, we imply that our love has
limitations. Today make a choice to spread
life. Spread love!

A Crop of Love

*"I said, 'Plant the good seeds
of righteousness, and you
will harvest a crop of love.' "*

HOSEA 10:12 NLT

Imagine yourself as a farmer out in the field planting good seeds. What sort of crop do you think you will yield? An awesome one, no doubt! Harvesting love is much like that. When we start with the right attitude and a heart for God and others, love always follows. We need to start with softened hearts, though, so spend some time today asking the Lord to break up the hard places.

A Love That Remains

"Remain in me, as I also remain in you.
No branch can bear fruit by itself; it
must remain in the vine. Neither can
you bear fruit unless you remain in me."

JOHN 15:4 NIV

Want to know how to have a love that
remains? One that will never die? Remain
in the Lord. Abide in Him. If you're in a
fruitless season of your life, double-check to
make sure you're still connected to the Life
Giver. Once you're grafted into the vine,
fruit will grow—and love will flow!

Love—Active and Fruitful

Love, like truth and beauty, is concrete.
Love is not fundamentally a sweet
feeling; not, at heart, a matter of
sentiment, attachment, or being
"drawn toward." Love is active,
effective, a matter of making reciprocal
and mutually beneficial relation
with one's friends and enemies.

CARTER HEYWARD

What do you suppose would happen if you neglected love? If you never used it? If you hid it away from others? Love is active. It's meant to be shown. Used. Given. Received. It's not what we feel; it's what we do. And it's not just meant to be shared among friends and loved ones. No, "active" love spills over onto others—in the workplace, in the grocery store, even when we're driving!

Love—a Choice

It's Your Choice

*"If you refuse to serve the LORD,
then choose today whom you will serve."*

JOSHUA 24:15 NLT

What a wonderful privilege that we get to
choose so many things in life! We choose
whom we marry, where we live, what church
we go to, what clothes we wear. Above all
of those things, however, is life's most
important choice: choosing to serve the
Lord. Today He reaches out with arms of
love. Will you respond to that love? It's your
choice.

Dress for Success

And over all these virtues put on love,
which binds them all together
in perfect unity.

COLOSSIANS 3:14 NIV

Have you ever considered that love is part
of your wardrobe? In the same way that you
slip on a blouse or a pair of slacks, you can
dress yourself in love each day. Adding love
to the wardrobe means you're truly dressed
for success. It's not always easy. In fact, you
have to choose to wear love, much as you
would choose your shoes. It's always the
right choice!

Let Love Flow!

"Just as the Father has loved Me, I have also loved you; abide in My love."

JOHN 15:9 NASB

We love as we are loved. Think about that statement for a minute. We tend to share love to the same degree that we receive it. God pours out His love to us 24/7. His fountain of grace, love, and mercy flows freely. And as long as we continue to drink from that fountain, we will become a wellspring of life for others. Abide in Him. Let love flow!

A Moment-to-Moment Choice

*Love is a choice you make
from moment to moment.*

BARBARA DE ANGELIS

Can you hear the ticking of the clock as the seconds pass by? Blink and another second is gone! Turn your head for a moment and you've lost it. In just that amount of time—a blink of an eye—you can choose to love. It is a choice, you know. You can choose to love even the most unlovable person. Don't let another minute tick by. Choose love.

A Necklace of Love

Let love and faithfulness never leave you; bind them around your neck, write them on the tablet of your heart. Then you will win favor and a good name in the sight of God and man.

PROVERBS 3:3–4 NIV

Have you ever had a really great necklace? Perhaps a relative or close friend has passed one down to you. In some ways, love is like an exquisite necklace, one you deliberately choose to wear. Each bead or stone represents one person you've loved or someone you've forgiven. It encircles you, reminding you of God's endless love. And it hangs near your heart, a constant reminder that He is only a heartbeat away.

Love as He Loves

Because He First Loved Me

Whoever does not love their brother and sister, whom they have seen, cannot love God, whom they have not seen. And they have given us this command: Whoever loves God must also love their brother and sister.

1 John 4:20–21 NIV

Can you imagine anything more frustrating to the unbeliever than a Christian who claims to love God but doesn't extend love—or mercy, or grace—to others? How hypocritical that must seem. Those who follow Jesus Christ are called to share His love, and not just to people who seemingly deserve it. Jesus loved the unlovable, and we're called to do the same. Following wholeheartedly after God means we must love as He loves.

As I Have Loved You

"A new commandment I give to you,
that you love one another,
even as I have loved you,
that you also love one another."

JOHN 13:34 NASB

Why do you suppose Jesus had to command
His followers to love one another? Seems a
little sad, doesn't it? You would think that
loving others would come naturally. But Jesus
realizes we don't always have it in us to offer
the same kind of love that He offers. His love
is life-changing. Oh, that we could extend
life-changing love to the world around us!

27

A Sweet-Smelling Offering

*Live a life of love just as Christ
loved us and gave himself for us
as a sweet-smelling offering
and sacrifice to God.*

EPHESIANS 5:2 NCV

What does it mean to live a life of love?
For some it comes naturally. Others have
to work at it! Living a life of love means
that you pour yourself out like perfume as a
fragrant offering—both to God and to those
around you. Your words taste and smell
sweet. So do your actions. You leave behind
a pleasant aroma, and people long to be
around you. Mmm! Smell that love?

Slow to Anger

The LORD is compassionate and gracious, slow to anger, abounding in love. He will not always accuse, nor will he harbor his anger forever; he does not treat us as our sins deserve or repay us according to our iniquities.

PSALM 103:8–10 NIV

One way to know you're "abounding" in God's love is to live a life that reflects His character. When you're slow to anger and refuse to knee-jerk when provoked, you're demonstrating His love. God doesn't treat us as we deserve (thank goodness!), and He expects that we will offer that same generosity to others, even when they wrong us. Don't repay evil for evil. Put the brakes on that anger!

Love's Measurement

Love measures our stature: the more we love, the bigger we are. There is no smaller package in all the world than that of a man all wrapped up in himself.

WILLIAM SLOANE COFFIN JR.

How big is your love? Think about that question for a moment. Do you "love big," or are you someone who holds back, only extending love when you feel it's deserved? When we withhold love, we're telling others that our thoughts and emotions are more important than they are. Love big today! Don't make everything all about you. You'll be surprised at how big you feel when you share God's love with others!

The Real Deal

The Love Proof

Dear children, let us not love with words or speech but with actions and in truth.

1 JOHN 3:18 NIV

It's one thing to tell people that you love them; it's another to live out that love with your actions. Sure, we say "I love you" all the time, but do we always follow those words up with the proof? Slipping up is easy, especially with people who are difficult to love. But God is always more interested in our actions than our words. He desires for us to love in word—and in deed.

Simple. . .and Difficult

Love one another and you will be happy.
It's as simple and as difficult as that.

MICHAEL LEUNIG

When you were young, you probably never thought of love as being difficult. It was as simple as wrapping your arms around your mother's neck or kissing your father good night. In the grown-up world, you discovered that some people are tough to love. Still, God commands it. Why? To test us? No, He longs for us to experience true joy, which comes only in a life filled with God-breathed love.

Nothing. . .
or Everything?

*If I speak in the tongues of men
or angels, but do not have love,
I am only a resounding gong or a
clanging cymbal. . .and if I have
a faith that can move mountains, but
do not have love, I am nothing.*

1 CORINTHIANS 13:1–2 NIV

It's one thing to claim to know God and to be called to a life of service to Him. It's another thing to back it up by loving the people He's placed in your life. You don't want to be a clanging gong (someone who talks the talk but doesn't walk the walk). Instead, be known as one who backs up her words with genuine love and compassion for others.

Forced to Love

Flatter me, and I may not believe you.
Criticize me, and I may not like you.
Ignore me, and I may not forgive you.
Encourage me, and I will not forget you.
Love me, and I may be forced
to love you.

WILLIAM ARTHUR WARD

Want to know how to win over even the toughest person? Win him with your love. Draw her with your kindness. People don't respond well to criticism or flattery, but love will win them every time. Oh, it might take awhile, especially if they don't trust you. But in the end, God-ordained love will usually win over even the toughest of people!

Genuine Love

You must teach people to have genuine love, as well as a good conscience and true faith.

1 TIMOTHY 1:5 CEV

Isn't it interesting to read that we have to "teach" people to have genuine love? You would think it would come naturally! But genuine love is tougher than it's advertised to be. Real love is, after all, sacrificial. We enjoy a kiss on the cheek or a hurried "I love you" as we're hanging up the phone. But sacrifice? That's not as easy, is it? Allow genuine love to lead the way today!

God's Love for Us

His Profound Love

*I pray that you, being rooted and
established in love, may have power,
together with all the Lord's holy people, to
grasp how wide and long and high and deep
is the love of Christ, and to know this love
that surpasses knowledge—that
you may be filled to the measure
of all the fullness of God.*

EPHESIANS 3:17–19 NIV

Have you ever paused to contemplate
God's unfathomable love for us? If we could
climb to the top of the highest mountain, we
couldn't outclimb His love. If we plummeted
to the depths, His love would meet us there.
If our vision could expand to see beyond the
stars, we would find His love waiting there
for us. There is truly nothing to compare
with the profound love of our Savior!

Shackles of Love

*There's nothing more freeing
than the shackles of love.*

EMMA RACINE DE FLEUR

God never intended that we should
live a life feeling imprisoned by anger,
frustration, or pain. Love overcomes all
of those things! In a manner of speaking,
love binds and shackles us, but we don't
feel imprisoned. Instead, we are set free!
God's love supersedes even the toughest
of challenges and tears down prison walls.
Today make a choice to replace the negative
shackles in your life with the shackles of
love.

Hearts Filled with Love

And this hope will not lead to disappointment. For we know how dearly God loves us, because he has given us the Holy Spirit to fill our hearts with his love.

ROMANS 5:5 NLT

Have you ever doubted God's love for you? Wondered if He's still there, looking out for you? One way you can know for sure that God loves you is to recognize His gift of the Holy Spirit, who resides inside you. God sent the Spirit, our Comforter, so that we would know we're never alone. Talk about a precious reminder of God's love!

Never Forsaken

For the LORD loves the just and will not forsake his faithful ones. Wrongdoers will be completely destroyed; the offspring of the wicked will perish.

PSALM 37:28 NIV

God loves all of humankind, but it's clear that He has a special place in His heart for those who call Him "Father." He adores those who are faithful to Him and who treat others justly. Unlike some earthly fathers, God never abandons His kids. Never. He will protect us forever. What an amazing heart of love our Daddy God has for us!

Abiding Love

*Whoever confesses that Jesus is the
Son of God, God abides in him, and he
in God. So we have come to know and
to believe the love that God has for us.
God is love, and whoever abides in love
abides in God, and God abides in him.*

1 JOHN 4:15–16 ESV

Are you wowed by God's unending love?
It's pretty amazing, isn't it? Once we
discover it—and see that it has no limits—we
are awed by such spectacular love! All we
have to do to receive this love is confess that
Jesus is the Son of God. When we do, the
Creator of heaven and earth sweeps in and
abides in us. Praise the Lord for His abiding
love!

Our Love for God

With All My Heart, Soul, and Mind

"You shall love the Lord your God with all your heart and with all your soul and with all your mind. This is the great and first commandment."

MATTHEW 22:37–38 ESV

It's one thing to love God with our heart. It's another to love Him with our mind. To love God with your mind means your ultimate desire is for His thoughts to be your thoughts. Spend some time focusing on loving God with your thoughts today. The reward will be great!

Because We Love Him

"Because he loves me," says the LORD,
*"I will rescue him; I will protect him,
for he acknowledges my name."*

PSALM 91:14 NIV

Have you fallen in love with the God of the universe? He desires a love relationship with you, you know. He longs for you to come into His presence and to give your heart to Him. When God sees that you've fallen head over heels for Him, He rushes in to become your rescuer and protector. This is love's response—to sweep in and protect. Oh, the powerr of love!

Faithful in Love

Love the LORD, all his faithful people!
The LORD preserves those who are true
to him, but the proud he pays
back in full.

PSALM 31:23 NIV

Being faithful is a natural consequence of loving someone. Because we love our spouse, we're faithful, no matter the temptation. And we stick by our family members, even when we disagree with their actions. We're true to our friends in thick and thin. God wants us to be faithful to Him as well. No straying. No playing the field. We're His bride, linked by love, faithful until He calls us home to heaven.

Showered with Grace

May God's grace be eternally upon all who love our Lord Jesus Christ.

EPHESIANS 6:24 NLT

Did you know that your love for Jesus has an amazing return? When you love Him, God showers you with grace, not just now, but for eternity. Grace, mercy, and compassion are yours—all because you love Him. What a great deal! Praise the Lord for His love-induced grace!

Loving Equals Giving

You can give without loving,
but you can never love without giving.

AUTHOR UNKNOWN

Isn't it interesting to think that God owns everything? Every star. Every continent. Every breath we breathe. He owns it all. Our time on earth is brief and we "own" so little in comparison with God, but what we do have, the Lord expects us to share. He wants us to be givers. When we're in relationship with others, we give to them—not out of obligation, but out of love, for loving equals giving.

Ah, Romance!

First Love

How on earth are you ever going to explain in terms of chemistry and physics so important a biological phenomenon as first love?

ALBERT EINSTEIN

Remember that feeling you got in the pit of your stomach the first time you "fell in love"? Felt like a butterfly farm had been set free, didn't it? You couldn't walk straight, talk straight, or think clearly. The only thing you could see was that other person. Most of us have long since forgotten about our first loves, but God has not. From the very beginning, He has been passionately in love with us!

46

Friendship Caught on Fire

Love is like a friendship caught on fire. In the beginning a flame, very pretty, often hot and fierce, but still only light and flickering. As love grows older, our hearts mature and our love becomes as coals, deep-burning and unquenchable.

BRUCE LEE

Isn't that an interesting quote? The best love relationships are based on strong friendship. When the two of you get along on multiple levels, you move beyond the "goose bumps and tingles" stage and into something more lasting. And how beautiful love looks as you grow old together. It's like a fire well tended, your love burning as deep as unquenchable coals. Oh, to have that kind of love!

Arise, My Love

My beloved spoke and said to me,
"Arise, my darling, my beautiful one,
come with me. See! The winter is past;
the rains are over and gone.
Flowers appear on the earth;
the season of singing has come. . . .
Arise, come, my darling; my beautiful
one, come with me."
SONG OF SONGS 2:10–13 NIV

There's something rather magical about finding real love. You know when it's right. If you've experienced a proposal of marriage, then you know what it's like to have that person extend a "Come away with me, my darling, my beautiful one" moment. Nothing in the earthly realm can top it. If you haven't experienced it, don't fret! God whispers those same words in your ear, even now. "Arise, my darling!"

For the Rest of My Life

When you realize you want to spend the rest of your life with somebody, you want the rest of your life to start as soon as possible.

Nora Ephron,
When Harry Met Sally

Oh, what bliss to discover the person you're supposed to marry! God designed men and women to love for a lifetime. And once you realize you've found "Mr. Right" (or Ms. Right), you're ready to jump in headfirst. This same kind of enthusiastic love was evidenced to us through the life of Jesus, who rushed headlong toward the cross. There He demonstrated a love that would never end.

His Banner over
Me Is Love

*"He has brought me to his banquet
hall, and his banner over me is love."*

SONG OF SOLOMON 2:4 NASB

Remember the song from childhood: "His
banner over me is love!" The only love that
comes close in this lifetime is the love found
between a husband and wife. When the
two are joined as one, you enter a "banquet
hall," where two become one in every sense
of the word. There, in that intimate place,
you share all of life's joys and sorrows—
together.

Loving Your Spouse

As You Love Yourself

Each one of you also must love his wife as he loves himself, and the wife must respect her husband.

EPHESIANS 5:33 NIV

Husbands are taught by scripture to love their wives as they love themselves. There's nothing more motivating to a wife than the genuine love of a godly husband, one who would be willing to lay down his life for her. It propels her to be the best possible wife she can be. Respect comes easy for a man who loves like that!

Love's Progression

Love seems the swiftest, but it is the slowest of all growths. No man or woman really knows what perfect love is until they have been married a quarter of a century.

MARK TWAIN

Ah, those first few years of marriage. We're blissfully, blindly in love. We can't see each other's flaws. But the passage of time brings everything to light, doesn't it? Our love shifts and progresses to something different altogether. No longer is it just about the "ooey, gooey" kind of love. Mature love now sees the flaws of the other person—but loves anyway. Now, that's real love!

Incomprehensible Love

There are three things that amaze me—no, four things that I don't understand: how an eagle glides through the sky, how a snake slithers on a rock, how a ship navigates the ocean, how a man loves a woman.

PROVERBS 30:18–19 NLT

The love between a man and woman is a wondrous thing. It's God-breathed. When two people are in love, they can't see straight. Nothing else exists! God designed us to share this amazing, toe-tapping, heart-singing love. It's inexplicable and often defies reason, but that's the beauty of it. Some things just aren't meant to be understood only experienced.

She Who Loves Her Husband. . .

These older women must train the younger women to love their husbands and children.

TITUS 2:4 NLT

In biblical times, young women often married older men, and not usually for love. They were betrothed based on a selection made by the father. No wonder they would have to "train" to love their husbands! Love would grow over time after the couple took their vows. Things are different today, but we all still need time to mature in our love. Real love continues to grow over time.

Gazing the Same Direction

Love does not consist of gazing at each other, but in looking together in the same direction.

ANTOINE DE SAINT-EXUPERY

When you're in love with someone, you often find yourself staring into each other's eyes. Ah, love! It's so romantic. People who've been in love for many years, however, learn that it's far more important to gaze in the same direction—toward the Lord. Keeping our eyes on Him will keep the romance fresh and the direction sure.

Loving Your Family

Morning Dew

Love is like dew that falls on both nettles and lilies.

SWEDISH PROVERB

Not every person is easy to love, even within our families. There's usually at least one member of the clan who presents an ongoing challenge. Here's the good news: God's love really does rain down on those who are easy to love—and on those who aren't. And because we recognize that He loves everyone, we can open our hearts to love them, too—easy or not.

Love in the House

Better a small serving of vegetables with love than a fattened calf with hatred.

PROVERBS 15:17 NIV

We often think that material possessions can buy happiness. Nothing is further from the truth. What good would it serve if you had everything but couldn't get along with the people in your own household? How sad that would be. It would be better to toss the fancy car and expensive house and learn to love your family the way God loves them. It might be challenging, but the end result would make it all worthwhile.

Love for Children

Before becoming a mother I had a hundred theories on how to bring up children. Now I have seven children and only one theory: Love them, especially when they least deserve to be loved.

KATE SAMPERI

Remember the first time you gazed down into the face of your baby? Oh, the feelings of love that swept over you. Then that little darling turned two and learned the word *no*. Suddenly love got mixed up with discipline and you found yourself a little short-tempered. Loving your child is easy—most of the time. But even in the challenging moments, remember that we're God's kids, and His love for us never ceases!

Saved by Love

By faith Noah, when warned
about things not yet seen, in holy
fear built an ark to save his family.
By his faith he condemned the world
and became heir of the righteousness
that is in keeping with faith.

HEBREWS 11:7 NIV

There's a great story in the Bible
about Noah—a righteous man chosen
by God to save humankind by building
an ark. Noah and his family climbed
aboard the monstrous boat and escaped
the floodwaters. Why did God choose
Noah? Because he was a righteous man.
Humankind was saved by God's love, not
just on the ark, but when God sent His
Son, Jesus, to rescue us from sin.

The Need for Love

*A baby is born with a need
to be loved—
and never outgrows it.*

FRANK A. CLARK

Ever wondered what your child needs? A new toy? The latest, greatest video game? A fancy house? The best school? Perfect parents? No, the one thing your child needs above all is love. That's it, plain and simple. When they're good, and when they're bad, our children need to see consistent, God-breathed love—from their parents, grandparents, teachers, and friends. Spend time loving a child today. You won't regret it, and neither will the child!

Loving Your Neighbor

Sum It Up!

The commandments, "You shall not commit adultery," "You shall not murder" and whatever other command. . . there may be, are summed up in this one command: "Love your neighbor as yourself."

ROMANS 13:9 NIV

Love your neighbor as yourself." We've heard these familiar words all of our lives, but what do they mean? And who is our neighbor? The guy in the house next door? The woman at the grocery store? Our neighbors are those people we see day in and day out. God desires that we love them in the very same way we love ourselves. Today ask the Lord to show you how to love your neighbors.

Around the Clock Love

A friend loves at all times, and a brother is born for a time of adversity.

PROVERBS 17:17 NIV

Have you ever considered the idea that a friend loves at all times? Seems impossible, doesn't it? Even friends squabble. They don't get along from time to time. They might even part ways. Still, God longs for the love to remain intact. Today if you're in a rough season with a friend, ask the Lord to restore your love. Then be ready to be that person's friend—24/7.

Brotherly Affection

Let love be genuine. Abhor what is evil;
hold fast to what is good. Love one
another with brotherly affection.
Outdo one another in showing honor.

ROMANS 12:9–10 ESV

Brotherly affection is that "slap on the back," "laugh at the same jokes" kind of love. Affection means caring. When you love, you genuinely care about other people—how they feel, their hopes and dreams, their heartbreaks. Everything about them matters to you because it matters to them. Hold fast to what is good. Love one another!

Love Your Brother

Whoever claims to love God yet hates a brother or sister is a liar. For whoever does not love their brother and sister, whom they have seen cannot love God, whom they have not seen. And he has given us this command: Anyone who loves God must also love their brother and sister.

1 JOHN 4:20–21 NIV

It's interesting to think that we're commanded to love God even though we have never seen Him with our eyes. Stranger still is that we have a hard time loving our brother—friend, neighbor, fellow church member—whom we *have* seen. God's ideal arrangement includes loving both the one we can see and the One we can't.

Plural Love

Love is not singular except in syllable.
MARVIN TAYLOR

Love is plural. It's not an "I, me, my" thing. It's meant to be shared among two or more parties. Whether you share it with a spouse, parent, child, neighbor, or friend at church, when you give love, you receive love. When you share it, you double your portion. And when you love others, you receive love in response. Thank God for love's plurality!

Loving Your Enemies

Love Your Enemies

"But I say, love your enemies!
Pray for those who persecute you!"
MATTHEW 5:44 NLT

We're not just called to love people who love us; we're commanded to love the ones who hurt us—the very ones who bring us grief. How is that possible? First, we have to acknowledge that all of us sin and fall short of the glory of God. Next, we have to let go of any bitterness and pain. Finally, we must pray for our enemies. Only in prayer can love win out.

The Love Test

*If your enemy is hungry, give him
bread to eat, and if he is thirsty,
give him water to drink, for you will
heap burning coals on his head,
and the LORD will reward you.*

PROVERBS 25:21–22 ESV

What would you do if your mortal enemy
was in trouble? Say, his house burned down
or his child was critically ill? Would you
pass the love test? Could you lay your angst
aside and extend a hand in his direction,
genuinely offering love? Spend some time
today asking the Lord to share His plan
for sharing love with those who have
become enemies. Before long, the
walls will come tumbling down!

A Directed Heart

*May the Lord direct your hearts
into the love of God and into
the steadfastness of Christ.*

2 Thessalonians 3:5 nasb

God longs for us to be directed, not by
emotion, but by His love and the steadfastness of His Son. When we allow our
hearts to be directed by God's amazing love,
we really can deal with our enemies in a
godly way. We have to slow down, take a deep
breath, and listen for God's voice. Only then
can we sense His direction and respond with
His love leading the way.

Love. . .and Do Good

*"But to you who are listening I say:
Love your enemies, do good
to those who hate you."*

LUKE 6:27 NIV

Love is always followed by actions. And not just any actions, either. When we genuinely love someone, we will respond to him with kindness. We'll treat him right, even if he doesn't respond similarly. Love always goes hand in hand with "doing good." Sure, it's hard at times, but God will give you the strength to get through, so dive in! Loving others with your actions is the way to go!

Transformed by Love

Love is the only force capable of transforming an enemy into a friend.

MARTIN LUTHER KING JR.

Love is a powerful force, bringing mortal enemies together and restoring near-impossible relationships. Think of someone you've fallen out of relationship with. Take the time to pray for him or her. Ask the Lord to show you how to love that person so that the relationship can be restored if at all possible. Then sit back and wait for the transformation to take place!

Love for Your Fellow Believers

Love for the Church

*We know that we have passed out of death
into life, because we love the brothers.
Whoever does not love abides in death.*

1 JOHN 3:14 ESV

Our brothers and sisters in Christ should
be like family members to us. And like family
members, they're not always easy to love! But
loving fellow church members is the best way
to show that we love God. If we love Him, we
should love His kids. This is how we know that
we are alive in Christ.

71

Love's Meditation

Within your temple, O God,
we meditate on your unfailing love.
PSALM 48:9 NIV

Don't you just love corporate worship?
There's something about lifting your voice,
your hands, and your heart to the King of
kings and Lord of lords in the midst of
fellow believers. And what an awesome
time to meditate on God's unfailing love.
As one body, one unit, we come together and
recognize the very love that binds us.
How wonderful to dwell together—in love!

Loving His People

God is always fair. He will remember how you helped his people in the past and how you are still helping them. You belong to God, and he won't forget the love you have shown his people.

HEBREWS 6:10 CEV

God is watching to see how we treat fellow believers. He's looking down from His throne in heaven, making sure we're bound together by His love. When we love, we extend a hand of kindness and friendship. No, it's not always easy, but it's God's way. And isn't it interesting to read that God won't forget how we've helped His people? His long-term memory is wonderful!

Brothers and Sisters

Respect everyone, and love your
Christian brothers and sisters.
Fear God, and respect the king.

1 PETER 2:17 NLT

Families have squabbles even under the best of circumstances. The same holds true in the body of Christ. We're one big happy family with God as our Father, but sometimes we disagree. We even argue. Loving someone doesn't mean you'll always see eye to eye, but it does mean you respect the other person and treat him or her with dignity. Now, that's God's kind of love!

Supreme Happiness

The supreme happiness of life
is the conviction that we are loved—
loved for ourselves, or rather,
loved in spite of ourselves.

VICTOR HUGO

Stumbling through life without love would be so difficult. There's nothing better than realizing you're loved simply because you're you. You don't have to do anything to earn it. You're simply loved. Doesn't that make your heart want to sing? God loves us in spite of ourselves! Praise Him for that!

Responding to Your Coworkers in Love

Built Up by Love

Knowledge puffs up while love builds up.
1 CORINTHIANS 8:1 NIV

If you're active in the workforce, then you know how tough it can be to love your fellow workers. More often than not, we're out to prove that we're better than the next person, not to shower that person with love. However, sharing God's love with others at our workplace is really God's plan for us. Make a decision today to build up your coworkers by loving them.

What the World Needs

What the world really needs is more love and less paperwork.

PEARL BAILEY

Ah, the office! Sometimes chaos reigns. The workload is high, stresses are even higher, and emotions rule the day. In the midst of the deadline-infused madness, we're expected to love our coworkers, not just in word, but also in deed. Seem impossible? It's not. We need to stop long enough to take a deep breath and focus. With God's help, even the madness is manageable, as long as we allow His love to lead the way.

Our Pursuit

Whoever pursues righteousness and love
finds life, prosperity and honor.

PROVERBS 21:21 NIV

Want to be respected in the workplace? Want to garner the right attention from coworkers and the boss? Try righteousness and love. Stand up for what's right. If you pursue righteousness (even when others around you are succumbing to temptation), and if you genuinely love your fellow workers, you will come out a winner in the end. No, the road won't always be easy, but it will be worth it.

Loved Back

Love life and life will love you back.
Love people and they will love you back.

ARTHUR RUBINSTEIN

In the workplace, we often see the best
and the worst in people. Some are almost
impossible to get along with. We pour out
love, and they don't respond. We try again
and receive nothing. We cry out, "How can I
love this person? I don't even like him!" If
you're dealing with a "tough case," don't give
up. Keep extending love. The payoff may
be delayed, but you will be found faithful
in the meantime.

A Growing Love

Dear brothers and sisters, we can't help but thank God for you, because your faith is flourishing and your love for one another is growing.

2 THESSALONIANS 1:3 NLT

Sometimes office relationships can wane over time. Maybe you start out as friends, but the stresses of the environment cause a deterioration in the friendship. If you want to maintain great interoffice friendships that grow even stronger with time, you have to keep brotherly love in the forefront. It won't always be easy, but it will be worth it.

Love for the Nations

Good News for
the Nations!

This same Good News that came to you is going out all over the world. It is bearing fruit everywhere by changing lives, just as it changed your lives.

COLOSSIANS 1:6 NLT

The word *gospel* means good news. We have good news for the nations! Jesus Christ came and gave His life for all! If you had great news that affected your children or friends, wouldn't you share it? Of course you would. The same holds true with the nations. When we develop a love for the nations (and this is God's heart for us all as believers), we can't help but share the good news.

Hope for the Nations

*In his name the nations
will put their hope.*

MATTHEW 12:21 NIV

Hope. What a wonderful, precious commodity. When we have hope, we can face today—and tomorrow. And when we have a love for God's people across the planet, even in places where we've never been, we long to offer them hope as well. But who will share the Good News? We're all called to participate! Through our giving, our "going," and our great love, the gospel will be spread.

Disciple the Nations

*Therefore go and make disciples of
all nations, baptizing them in the
name of the Father and of the Son
and of the Holy Spirit.*

MATTHEW 28:19 NIV

To truly disciple people, we have to love
them. Otherwise, we won't go the distance
with them. It's a day-in, day-out process
that can be grueling. We're commanded
by Jesus to go and make disciples of all
nations—not converts, but disciples. Love
compels us to go the distance by offering
financial support to missionaries or by
making the commitment to go
ourselves. Today pray about the role
you play in reaching the nations.

Every Knee Will Bow

It is written: " 'As surely as I live,'
says the Lord, 'every knee will bow
before me; every tongue will
acknowledge God.' "

ROMANS 14:11 NIV

Can you imagine what it will be like on
that day when every knee bows and every
tongue confesses that Jesus Christ is Lord?
Oh, what joy that will be! May our love for
God and our love for His people motivate
us to reach the unreached people groups of
the world. Every day we're one step closer to
that glorious day!

The Hunger for Love

The hunger for love is much more difficult to remove than the hunger for bread.

MOTHER TERESA

Don't you love that quote by Mother Teresa? She's right. People all over the world crave love. Many don't even realize that's what they're longing for. We have the love they need. By sharing Christ, we're passing on the greatest gift of all—His redemptive love. And when we extend a hand—with food, fellowship, compassion, and prayer—we're adding our love to His. We have the power to quench the world's spiritual hunger.

Love as a Witness

By This All People Will Know

"Just as I have loved you, you also are to love one another. By this all people will know that you are my disciples, if you have love for one another."

JOHN 13:34–35 ESV

The Bible says that people will know we're God's kids by our love. Love itself is our greatest witness. It's even more important than sharing the gospel or laying out the four spiritual laws. Those things are important, but love is still the key. We back up our words with our actions. And when we love others—truly love them—our words are much more palatable.

Singing of His Love

I will sing of the LORD's great love forever; with my mouth I will make your faithfulness known through all generations. I will declare that your love stands firm forever, that you have established your faithfulness in heaven itself.

PSALM 89:1–2 NIV

When you're filled with the love of the Lord, it's hard to contain the song that rises up in your heart. Why stop it? Let it flow! Praise makes even the hardest situation manageable. And what a great witness! When others hear you humming, when they see your passion for praise, they will wonder what you have that they don't. Join in the great love song of all time today—praise to the King of kings!

The Ways to Love

I truly feel that there are as many
ways of loving as there are people
in the world and as there are days
in the lives of those people.

MARY S. CALDERONE

We all have different love languages, don't
we? For some, giving of one's time is the
most important thing. For others it's gift
giving. Some respond well to acts of service,
and still others to words of encouragement
and praise. If you're trying to witness to a
friend or neighbor, take the time to learn
that person's love language first. Then love
that person as she or he needs to be loved.

Directed by Love

*May the Lord direct your hearts
into the love of God and into the
steadfastness of Christ.*

2 THESSALONIANS 3:5 NASB

It's interesting to read that God
occasionally needs to direct our hearts into
His love. Think about how you steer a car.
The steering wheel needs a little nudge to
the right or the left. That's how it is with
love, too. If we don't willingly accept God's
little nudges, our love for others can grow
cold. Keep your witness strong by allowing
the Lord to direct your heart as He sees fit.

The One I Love

*"Here is my servant whom I have
chosen, the one I love, in whom I
delight; I will put my Spirit on him, and
he will proclaim justice to the nations."*

MATTHEW 12:18 NIV

It's easier to be a good witness when we
realize that God has given us His Spirit. It
also helps to know that we're loved whether
we mess up or not. And we do mess up, don't
we! We set out to share God's love with a
friend and end up in an argument with her
instead. Ugh! Still, God loves us, and His
Spirit gives us the courage to go out and try
again.

Giving Out of Love

Loving Those in Need

If anyone has material possessions and sees a brother or sister in need but has no pity on them, how can the love of God be in that person?

1 JOHN 3:17 NIV

If we love God, we need to take care of others even if it means reaching into our wallets to do it. Material possessions are meant to be shared. They're a tool for ministering to others. People see our love when we take pity on them in their need. And when we give, our hearts are exposed. Love comes pouring out.

91

A Fragrant Offering

Christ loved us and gave himself up for us as a fragrant offering and sacrifice to God.

EPHESIANS 5:2 NIV

If we ever want to know how to give, all we have to do is follow God's example. He gave His only Son so that we would have life. Talk about a fragrant love offering! Giving is sacrificial, which means it isn't always pleasant. We have to remember that giving isn't about us. It's about our love for God and His people. Love is a great motivator to give.

Giving Thanks

" 'There will be heard once more
the sounds of joy and gladness, the
voices of bride and bridegroom,
and the voices of those who bring thank
offerings to the house of the LORD,
saying, "Give thanks to the LORD
Almighty, for the LORD is good; his
love endures forever." ' "

JEREMIAH 33:10–11 NIV

One of the ways we "give" is to give thanks to the Lord. How easy it is to forget to thank Him for His many blessings. When we see His love for us, when we realize that He's never going to leave us or forsake us, we're motivated to give thanks. And as we lift our voices in praise, others are watching. We're teaching them to offer words of thanks to God as well!

Excel in Giving

But just as you excel in everything—
in faith, in speech, in knowledge,
in complete earnestness and in the love
we have kindled in you—see that you
also excel in this grace of giving.

2 CORINTHIANS 8:7 NIV

We want to excel at everything we do, and that takes effort on our part. So we work to have excellent parenting skills. An excellent work ethic. Excellent financial prowess. But what about giving? If we love God and others, we should strive to become excellent givers. Want to excel today? Consider giving of yourself to others.

Never Wasted

Love and kindness are never wasted.
They always make a difference.
They bless the one who receives them,
and they bless you, the giver.

BARBARA DE ANGELIS

We don't give to get. Still, there's no denying that love is reciprocal. It has a boomerang effect. It's never wasted. What goes around comes around. Even if you're setting out to be a blesser, you'll end up being blessed in the end. And when you reach deep to give, the blessing can far outweigh the sacrifice.

His Love toward Us

For great is his love toward us,
and the faithfulness of the LORD
endures forever. Praise the LORD.

PSALM 117:2 NIV

We'll never be able to understand God's love toward us. It extends grace when grace is the last thing we deserve. It offers forgiveness when we've committed the most heinous of sins. It reaches out to us when we're haughty and proud and comes looking for us when we've sunk to the lowest low. Doesn't that kind of love make you feel like shouting? Like praising God at the top of your voice?

I Will Bow Down

*I will bow down toward your holy
temple and will praise your name
for your unfailing love and your
faithfulness, for you have
so exalted your solemn decree
that it surpasses your fame.*

PSALM 138:2 NIV

Sometimes we come into God's presence
and we feel like shouting for joy. At other
times His love drives us to our knees. Oh,
how we're humbled by what He has done for
us. We kneel in His presence and praise His
name, not just for His gifts, but also for His
moment-by-moment offering of love.
Our God is worthy to be praised!

A Poetic Heart

Poetry spills from the cracks of a broken heart, but flows from one which is loved.

CHRISTOPHER PAUL RUBERO

When we're broken and bruised, we turn inward. The pain leaks from the cracks like a melancholy dirge. But when we're aware of God's goodness toward us—His love, His grace, His mercy—a different sort of song erupts. We're overcome with a melody of praise!

Rejoicing in Love

Rejoice in His Love!

*I will be glad and rejoice in your love,
for you saw my affliction and knew
the anguish of my soul.*

PSALM 31:7 NIV

Are you one of those people who loves to praise God? Do you enjoy lifting your heart and voice to Him in glorious song for all He's done? The Lord loves it when His children offer a sacrifice of praise. And why not? His love provokes us to exalt Him. When we think about it, when we come to fully understand it, how can we do anything but praise?

Give Thanks to the Lord

*After consulting the people, Jehoshaphat appointed men to sing to the L*ORD *and to praise him for the splendor of his holiness as they went out at the head of the army, saying: "Give thanks to the* L*ORD, for his love endures forever."*

2 CHRONICLES 20:21 NIV

Don't you love early mornings? They're filled with promise. New day. New dawn. New chance to experience God's awesome love. He is pleased when we make a choice to give thanks early in the day. His enduring love never sleeps, so it meets us fresh every morning. Praise Him for that unfailing love, even before your eyes are fully open!

Sing for Joy

But let all who take refuge in you be glad; let them ever sing for joy. Spread your protection over them, that those who love your name may rejoice in you.

PSALM 5:11 NIV

There are so many things to rejoice over when you're in love with the Creator of heaven and earth. Rejoicing changes your perspective on everything! Remember that little song you used to sing as a child: "I've got the joy, joy, joy, joy down in my heart!" It's true. Love gives birth to joy. And when that joy spills over, watch out! It's contagious!

Those Who Love Salvation

*But may all who seek you rejoice
and be glad in you; may those who
long for your saving help always say,
"The LORD is great!"*

PSALM 40:16 NIV

When you think about what Jesus did on the cross for you, how does it make you feel? Overwhelmed? Grateful? Filled with joy? The free gift of salvation gives us all the reason we could ever need to lift our voices in praise to God. There on Calvary, He poured out His love for humankind. And now we have the glorious privilege of pouring out our praise in response.

God's Finger

*There is no surprise more magical
than the surprise of being loved.
It is God's finger on man's shoulder.*

CHARLES MORGAN

Have you ever had a surprise birthday party? Maybe the guests caught you off guard with the surprise celebration. God's love is a lot like that. When we least suspect it. . .surprise! He showers us with His love. When we're feeling as if we're completely unlovable. . .surprise! There He goes again, loving us unconditionally. Talk about a reason to praise!

Loving in Hard Times

Knowing God

*Whoever does not love does not know
God, because God is love.*

1 JOHN 4:8 NIV

Love isn't always easy, is it? Sometimes it's tough to extend love, particularly when our feelings are hurt or we're wounded in some way. The Bible is clear that God is love. He epitomizes it, in fact. And if we withhold our love from others, even if we feel justified, we break God's heart. If we claim to know Him, we have no choice but to love.

The Ride

Love doesn't make the world go 'round;
love is what makes the ride worthwhile.

FRANKLIN P. JONES

Likely you've heard the old expression: "Love makes the world go 'round." Truthfully, God makes the world go 'round, but He is love, after all! His love is the driving force in our lives, and it certainly encourages us to keep going, even when we don't feel like loving others. The next time you think you can't hang on for the ride, remember that God's love is strong enough to cover all the rocky places.

Love's Vision

Love is not blind—it sees more, not less.
But because it sees more,
it is willing to see less.

JULINS GORDON

When we walk in God's love, we have the power to see—and to overlook. Overlook what, you ask? Flaws in others. Slip-ups from those who make mistakes. Careless words spoken to us by others. When we love someone—truly love someone—we're able to see past the mess-ups and offer forgiveness. That's what it means to have God's vision.

Supported by Love

When I said, "My foot is slipping," your
unfailing love, LORD, supported me.
When anxiety was great within me,
your consolation brought me joy.

PSALM 94:18–19 NIV

Do you ever feel like slipping when you're around an unlovable person? Saying the wrong thing? Letting the other person have it? Some people really are harder to love than others, but God's brand of love guards itself against the slippery slope of anger. Next time you feel like snapping, ask the Lord for His perspective. He can refill your love tank in a hurry!

Because of His Great Love

*But because of his great love for us,
God, who is rich in mercy, made us
alive with Christ even when we were
dead in transgressions—it is by
grace you have been saved.*

EPHESIANS 2:4–5 NIV

Sometimes we just don't feel like loving.
We not only withhold love, but we punish
others by not forgiving them for what they
have done to us. This brings a rift in our
relationships, and it isn't good for us. Love
acts as a buffer. God extended mercy to us.
Why? Because of His great love. We must
love, even in the hard times, so that mercy
and grace can follow.

The Love Pursuit

Chasing After Love

*Whoever pursues righteousness and love
finds life, prosperity and honor.*

PROVERBS 21:21 NIV

Sometimes love comes easily, and at other times we have to pursue it. Chase after it. Catch up to it. When we pursue the Lord with our whole hearts, He will give us the ability to love even the most difficult people. That's the kind of compassion He showed us, after all. He pursued us all the way to the cross. Talk about a love pursuit!

Follow Hard after God

Take me away with you—let us hurry!
Let the king bring me into his chambers.

SONG OF SONGS 1:4 NIV

Have you ever heard the expression "follow hard after God"? To follow Him with passion means that you can't live without Him. This kind of passionate love between God and His people has been going on since the beginning of time. He longs for you to run into His arms so that His love can bring healing in your life. Hurry into His chambers today! There He awaits with arms extended.

Search and Find

"I love all who love me.
Those who search will surely find me."
PROVERBS 8:17 NLT

Isn't it wonderful to know that our love for God is always reciprocated? We express love. He returns it—and then some. Not so with humans! But God has the ability to return our love with interest! We could never outgive Him, no matter how hard we tried. If you're on a search for love, turn to the One who knows it best—and expresses it most.

Overflowing Love

*And may the Lord make your love for
one another and for all people
grow and overflow, just as our
love for you overflows.*

1 THESSALONIANS 3:12 NLT

Overfilling a glass can be messy; overfilling your love tank is anything but! God wants us to have overflowing love—for him, for our fellow believers, and even for those who annoy us. If you ask, the Lord will increase your love for others. Before long, you'll be spilling all over everyone—those you're closest to and those who drive you a little crazy!

Tend the Fire of Love

*Love is like a campfire:
It may be sparked quickly, and at first
the kindling throws out a lot of heat,
but it burns out quickly. For long-lasting,
steady warmth (with delightful bursts
of intense heat from time to time),
you must carefully tend the fire.*

MOLLEEN MATSUMURA

Part of the love pursuit is stirring the embers. We can't allow love to grow stagnant. Keeping it aflame requires work on our part. Think about the various love relationships in your life today. Your relationship with the Lord. Your love for family members, friends, and coworkers. Do any of those relationships need a good stirring? If so, get busy! Don't let that love-fire go out!

Love Lights the Way

The Most Excellent Way

I will show you the most excellent way. If I speak in the tongues of men or of angels, but do not have love, I am only a resounding gong or a clanging cymbal.

1 CORINTHIANS 12:31–13:1 NIV

If you've ever navigated a rocky path in the dark without a flashlight, you have some small taste of what it would be like to go through life without love. You could probably make it from point A to point B, but what a rough trip! In the scripture above, God shows us the most excellent way to make the journey. Let love light the way!

Guiding Light, Guiding Love

Love is not consolation. It is light.

FRIEDRICH NIETZSCHE

Don't you love the story of the wise men who followed the star to locate baby Jesus? The light guided them. Love is a lot like that. When it's burning brightly—and that's how God intended it to be—our vision is much clearer. We can see where we're going. It lights our path and guides us to our destination.

The Love Light

*Love must be as much
a light as it is a flame.*

HENRY DAVID THOREAU

Love brings warmth and comfort. It's like
a warm, cozy blanket on a cold day. But love
is as much a light as a flame. It's not just
meant to make us feel good. It sparks in our
innermost being and drives us to be better.
To care more. To share more. Love points
the way in every relationship, good and bad.

Faith, Hope, and Love

*Love never fails. . . . And now these
three remain: faith, hope and love.
But the greatest of these is love.*

1 CORINTHIANS 13:8, 13 NIV

When everything else fades away to
nothingness, love will remain. Think
about that for a moment. When this earth
as we know it is long gone, God's love for
us will remain. All of our possessions,
talents, and abilities will fade, but the way
we treated others—the love we showed
them—will linger forever in their memories.
Love people in such a way that they will
remember you long after you're gone.

Never a Waste

Loving is never a waste of time.
ASTRID ALAUDA

We waste a lot of time doing things that are frivolous. Playing video games, watching television, surfing the Internet, bickering with loved ones—these are all ways we fritter away the hours. Thankfully, loving others is never a waste of time. And what a great reflection of God! We illuminate the pathway for our children, friends, and other loved ones when we spend our days loving them.

The Love Debt

The Debt of Love

*Let no debt remain outstanding,
except the continuing debt to love
one another, for whoever loves
others has fulfilled the law.*

ROMANS 13:8 NIV

If you've ever taken out a loan for a car or
house, you know the woes of being indebted
to someone else. It's not a great feeling, is
it? There is one debt, however, that isn't
hard to carry. It's the debt of love. Anger
and strife can destroy relationships, but
when the debt of love is paid, hearts are
mended and pain is vanquished. May your
only debt be the debt of love!

Just Enough. . .to Love

*We have just enough religion
to make us hate, but not enough
to make us love one another.*

JONATHAN SWIFT

Throughout history, the church has struggled with the issue of love. Believers want unbelievers to line up and walk straight. To obey the commandments. To follow the letter of the law. Sometimes, though, we forget that extending love is the only way to win people to the Lord. May we forever be indebted to love, for it has the capacity to change hearts and lives.

"Feed My Lambs"

When they had finished eating, Jesus said to Simon Peter, "Simon son of John, do you love me more than these?" "Yes, Lord," he said, "you know that I love you." Jesus said, "Feed my lambs."

JOHN 21:15 NIV

What an earthshaking question Jesus asked Peter, His beloved disciple. "Peter, do you love Me more than these?" How would you answer that question? Surely you would cry out, as Peter did, "Yes, Lord! You know I do!" But Jesus' response to His followers will always be the same: "If you love Me, care for My children." We're forever indebted to love others in the body of Christ.

Happiness

*To love is to place our happiness
in the happiness of another.*

G. W. Von Leibnitz

We all want to be happy. In fact, most of us feel like we're "owed" happiness. True love, however, seeks the happiness of the other person. In some ways, we're indebted to the other person's well-being. That's God's way. We are to love others as we love ourselves. It's not always easy, but extending this kind of love has great benefits, for what goes around comes around. Seek happiness for others and you will receive it, too!

A Loving Proclamation

*"Therefore, my friends,
I want you to know that through
Jesus the forgiveness of sins
is proclaimed to you."*

ACTS 13:38 NIV

Through Jesus, God offers forgiveness of sins. Think about that for a minute. He has indebted Himself to humankind through Jesus' work on the cross. He paid the debt for our sin! In doing so, God has made a covenant with us: "Love My Son. Accept His free gift of salvation. In exchange, I will offer you forgiveness of sins and eternal life." Oh, what a gift! What a debt of love He paid!

Love of Life

"I Have Come That You Might Have Life"

A thief comes only to rob, kill, and destroy. I came so that everyone would have life, and have it in its fullest.

JOHN 10:10 CEV

Don't you just love life? It's filled with unexpected and undeserved joys. Sure, not every day is a piece of cake, but we're alive and well today and have hope for tomorrow. God's love for us is so deep that He came to earth so that we could have life. . .and not just any life. He wants us to have abundant life. That's a "more than I could ask or think" life.

Renewed by Love

*I love people. I love my family,
my children. . .but inside myself is a
place where I live all alone, and that's
where you renew your springs
that never dry up.*

PEARL S. BUCK

Where do you go to get renewed? To get
your love tank refilled? Sometimes we have
to escape the chaos—even the good chaos—
to find a place of quiet and rest inside
ourselves. We have to seek God in the secret
places so that we can be renewed by His
love. Otherwise, there won't be much inside
of us to give out.

Loving Life!

*Does anyone want to live a life
that is long and prosperous?
Then keep your tongue from speaking
evil and your lips from telling lies!*

PSALM 34:12–13 NLT

How blessed we are to be alive during the twenty-first century! We have much available to us and many things to enjoy. If you want to go on enjoying life for years to come, then spend your time loving others. Guard your tongue and treat people as you would like to be treated. Be honest in all you do. Your passion for life will increase as you speak words of love over others.

A Life of Devotion

The way you get meaning into your life is to devote yourself to loving others, devote yourself to your community around you, and devote yourself to creating something that gives you purpose and meaning.

MITCH ALBOM

If you're losing your enthusiasm or feeling down in the dumps, there's a surefire way to add excitement to your life. Love others. Devote yourself to them. Get outside of your "bubble" and focus on those around you in your community or church. Loving others will help you define your purpose and will reignite your passion for life!

Crowned with Love

Praise the LORD, my soul, and forget not all his benefits—who forgives all your sins and heals all your diseases, who redeems your life from the pit and crowns you with love and compassion.

PSALM 103:2–4 NIV

We take many things for granted in this life: our health, God's provision, our daily bread, the love of family members and friends, and much more. Oh, may we never forget to praise our loving God, who showers us with benefits. He forgives our sins. He redeems us from the pit. And He places a glittering crown of love and compassion on us, calling us His daughters and sons.

Ever-Abounding Love

Abounding...
More and More!

And it is my prayer that your love may abound more and more, with knowledge and all discernment, so that you may approve what is excellent, and so be pure and blameless for the day of Christ, filled with the fruit of righteousness that comes through Jesus Christ, to the glory and praise of God.

PHILIPPIANS 1:9–11 ESV

Have you ever watched a snowball roll down a hill? As it picks up speed, it begins to grow! Before long, it's huge and powerful! That's how love is. The more love you share, the more you get. The longer we love, the more we have the capacity to love. If you're hoping to receive more, try giving it away. Then get ready for the snowball effect!

131

Wealthy with His

And he passed in front of Moses, proclaiming, "The LORD, the LORD, the compassionate and gracious God, slow to anger, abounding in love and faithfulness."

EXODUS 34:6 NIV

Have you ever wondered what it means to be abounding in something? Try replacing the word *abounding* with the word *wealthy*. God is wealthy in love and faithfulness. He has more than enough to share with His kids. Talk about an inheritance! And He wants us to share the love. When we accept Jesus and walk in relationship with Him, we're wealthy with His love. Make a point to share the wealth today.

Resting in His Abounding Love

"Come to me, all you who are weary and burdened, and I will give you rest. Take my yoke upon you. . .for I am gentle and humble in heart, and you will find rest for your souls."

MATTHEW 11:28–31 NIV

If you're weary—exhausted with life—don't give up hope. God has a place of rest for those who are in relationship with Him. He woos us with His love, opening wide His arms and ushering us into His embrace. There we can hear His heartbeat. Get His perspective. Listen for His words of love, which energize us for the tasks ahead. Come, all you who are weary and heavy laden. Rest.

Love—a Living Thing

Love does not die easily. It is a living thing. It thrives in the face of all of life's hazards, save one—neglect.

JAMES D. BRYDEN

Love is a living, breathing thing. Our love for God and others is resilient. It can survive a host of onslaughts. One thing it can't survive, however, is neglect. We have to tend it. Care for it. Nurture it. If we follow God's example, our love will continue to abound, even when we're having an "off" day. Don't let those rough days keep you from nurturing love.

On the Rebound

But you, Lord, are a compassionate and gracious God, slow to anger, abounding in love and faithfulness.

PSALM 86:15 NIV

It's interesting to see that God's love is both abounding and rebounding. It keeps coming around to meet us again, even after we've failed. This is because of His compassionate nature. In the same way, we are expected to rebound (bounce back) even after our love for people is challenged. Don't stay away too long. Come back home to love.

Loving through Betrayal

A Savior Who Understands

While he was still speaking, there came
a crowd, and the man called Judas,
one of the twelve, was leading them.
He drew near to Jesus to kiss him.

LUKE 22:47 ESV

Have you ever been betrayed by someone you thought you could trust? Jesus can relate. Imagine how He must have felt watching one of the disciples He loved turn on Him and sell Him out for thirty pieces of silver. Perhaps you feel as if you've been sold out by a friend or loved one. Follow the example of Jesus, who, even in the face of betrayal, chose to forgive.

The Ultimate Betrayal

For while we were still weak, at the right time Christ died for the ungodly.

ROMANS 5:6 ESV

In spite of humankind's betrayal in the Garden of Eden, the Lord still chose to love us by sending His Son as a sacrifice for our sins. Even now, those of us who follow Jesus slip up and betray Him—with our actions, our thoughts, and our motives. How it must break God's heart! But still He offers love, in spite of His pain. What an amazing example for us to follow.

Covering Offenses

Hatred stirs up strife, but love covers all offenses.

PROVERBS 10:12 ESV

Once you've been betrayed, it's hard to trust again, isn't it? Sure. Trust needs to be reestablished, rebuilt over time. And our wounds need time to heal. But even when it's hard to trust, we have to keep on loving the person who betrayed us. Why? Because love and trust are two separate things. Trust has to be earned. Love does not. It covers offenses and tears down walls.

All Have Sinned

*For all have sinned and fall short
of the glory of God.*

ROMANS 3:23 NIV

One of the reasons it's so important for us
to continue loving those who have hurt us
is that we never know when it might be our
turn to be forgiven. Sure, we act out to do
the right thing, but even those with the best
of intentions slip up and hurt others. Extend
love and forgiveness at every turn. You never
know when it might be your turn to receive!

Heart Softener

Love is never lost. If not reciprocated,
it will flow back and soften
and purify the heart.

WASHINGTON IRVING

Sometimes we love someone to the point of pain but never receive love back. What does the Lord have to say about this? Should we stop trying? Stop loving? Never! Even if we don't see the desired results, love is always the better option. For when it is not reciprocated by the individual, it will always return to us in one form or another. Love never fails. People fall short, but love never does.

Forgiveness, Love's Key

Love Deeply

Above all, love each other deeply,
because love covers over a
multitude of sins.

1 PETER 4:8 NIV

It's human nature to withhold forgiveness in order to teach the other person a lesson, but that's not God's way. He doesn't want us to wait too long to forgive. His desire is that we're honest with each other when we're upset. After all, we all sin and fall short. We have to be willing to go the distance and do what it takes to mend fences. How do we accomplish this? Love deeply

Seeking After Love

*Whoever covers an offense seeks love,
but he who repeats a matter
separates close friends.*

PROVERBS 17:9 ESV

We don't get to pick our family members,
but we can select our friends. And when
we do, we're making a love pact with them.
In essence, we're saying: "We're in this
for the long haul. We will forgive quickly,
love deeply, and keep our conversations
private." Good friends seek after love, even
when times get tough. *Especially* when times
get tough.

Love Covers All Wrongs

"For this reason I say to you, her sins, which are many, have been forgiven, for she loved much; but he who is forgiven little, loves little."

LUKE 7:47 NASB

If you've ever been forgiven for something you considered really grievous, then you know what it means to be grateful! Love covers all wrongs. It also forgives on a grand scale. To extend this kind of forgiveness, you have to genuinely love the other person, both in word and in deed. Love big. Forgive big.

Prosperous Love

Love prospers when a fault is forgiven,
but dwelling on it separates
close friends.

PROVERBS 17:9 NLT

When we forgive someone who has wronged us, we're offering proof of our love. No, forgiving doesn't always mean reconciliation. Sometimes we need to separate for a season. Forgiveness doesn't imply an ongoing close relationship. God often calls friends and loved ones to take a sabbatical from each other. But love and forgiveness are still in order, even in the toughest situations.

Miraculous Love

Where there is great love,
there are always miracles.

WILLA CATHER

Do you believe in miracles? Have you witnessed them personally? God longs for us to see the miraculous on a regular basis. One area in which we witness the supernatural at work is in our relationships with others. Love-based forgiveness is truly miraculous. It says to the other person, "I know that you hurt me deeply, but I make a choice to extend forgiveness because I love you." What a miraculous gift!

Love and Prayer

A Love Song

By day the LORD directs his love,
at night his song is with me—
a prayer to the God of my life.

PSALM 42:8 NIV

Nighttime prayers are so precious. Our last words to God before our heads hit the pillow stir our hearts to praise through the night. And what a wonderful gift prayer is. It's an awesome privilege. We get to communicate with the Creator of all! We share our hurts, our pains, our joys, and our questions. Then the Lord responds by speaking to us, whispering words of love and direction.

Extending Love and Prayer

"But I tell you, love your enemies and pray for those who persecute you."

MATTHEW 5:44 NIV

We usually enjoy praying for others, as long as we're in good relationship with them. But this whole "Pray for your enemies" thing is tough! We don't want to ask God to bless our enemies. If we're honest, we're usually hoping for the opposite! But God commands us to love our enemies and to pray for them, too. So who's on your "enemy" list today? Better get busy!

No Love Withheld

*Praise be to God, who has not rejected
my prayer or withheld his love from me!*
PSALM 66:20 NIV

Sometimes we're afraid to pray because
we're upset with the Lord or others. We're
afraid that if we get gut-honest with God
in our prayers, He might reject us. Not so!
He will not withhold His love from us, even
when we're mad at Him! He's a big God.
He can take it. So get it out. Confess your
angst. Then watch as He sets everything
right again, with His amazing love leading
the way!

Praying. . .and Living

It is not well for a man to pray cream and live skim milk.

HENRY WARD BEECHER

During our prayer time, we often ask God to bless us. There's nothing wrong with that. We count on His love and blessings, but sometimes we don't want to extend those things to others. If we're going to ask for these things, then we have to be willing to give them to the people He places in our lives—even the ones who are most difficult to love!

A Confession of Love

*I prayed to the LORD my God
and confessed: "Lord, the great
and awesome God, who keeps his
covenant of love with those who love
him and keep his commandments."*

DANIEL 9:4 NIV

Prayer is such a wonderful gift. We get to talk to the King of kings and Lord of lords— and He responds! Our prayer time is also a wonderful time to thank God for His great love toward us. Why not spend some time praising Him today? Climb up into His lap and lean your head against His chest. Make a confession of your love for your Daddy God.

No Fear in Love

No Fear in Love

There is no fear in love. But perfect love drives out fear, because fear has to do with punishment. The one who fears is not made perfect in love.

1 JOHN 4:18 NIV

Oh, what a joy to know that love conquers fear. Think about that for a moment. When fear grips your heart, telling you that you're going to fail at something, God's love drives out that fear. It sends a calming message, one you can rest in. Next time fear slips in, remember it's not from God. He extends perfect love, the only force powerful enough to drive out fear!

Quieted by Love

*"The Lord your God is with you,
the Mighty Warrior who saves. He will
take great delight in you; in his love he
will no longer rebuke you, but will
rejoice over you with singing."*

ZEPHANIAH 3:17 NIV

If you're a parent, you know what it's like to rock a baby in your arms, calming him down so that he can sleep. Your words of love—sweetly sung—can quiet even the loudest squall. It's the same when we climb into God's arms. He quiets us with His love, calms our fears, and dries our eyes. We drift off to sleep with His gentle melody of love drifting over us.

Love Overcomes Timidity

For the Spirit God gave us does not make us timid, but gives us power, love and self-discipline.

2 TIMOTHY 1:7 NIV

Sometimes we're afraid to share our testimony with others or to talk about our faith. We're timid. We hold back. How wonderful to realize that God gave us a spirit of power, love, and self-discipline. With these three things firmly in place, we're able to open up and share the good news of His love.

Stouthearted Love

When I called, you answered me;
you greatly emboldened me.

PSALM 138:3 NIV

Love doesn't cower in fear. It holds its head up high and smiles in the face of a challenge. It cries out, "Be bold! Be strong!" If you're facing a fearful situation, call out to God. He will answer you and will give you the boldness you need to get through whatever situation you're facing.

Refreshed by Love

Love is the greatest refreshment in life.
PABLO PICASSO

Have you ever reached for a glass of lemonade on a hot day? It tastes so good, doesn't it? Hits the spot! Love is like that. When your friends and loved ones are parched and dry, they're not aching for a lecture. Instead, they're longing for a tall glass of love. Ah, sweet refreshment! Serve up a glass today.

Obedience

What God Requires

"And now, Israel, what does the LORD your God require of you, but to fear the LORD your God, to walk in all his ways, to love him, to serve the LORD your God with all your heart and with all your soul.".

DEUTERONOMY 10:12 ESV

It's fascinating to think that God "requires" us to love Him. More interesting still is that it's listed in this scripture, along with walking in his ways, fearing him, and serving him. These things work well together, and all the more when love is tucked in the middle. First we fear (respect) God; then we show our love by obeying Him; and that leads to a life of service.

Keep His Word

Jesus answered him, "If anyone loves me, he will keep my word, and my Father will love him, and we will come to him and make our home with him. Whoever does not love me does not keep my words. And the word that you hear is not mine but the Father's who sent me."

JOHN 14:23–24 ESV

Love and obedience have always walked hand in hand. If we love God, we will obey Him. Sure, our flesh doesn't always want to do it, but we'll have the best outcome if we stick with the teachings of the Bible and follow God's precepts to the best of our ability. Love equals obedience.

God Keeps His Covenant

"Understand, therefore, that the Lord your God is indeed God. He is the faithful God who keeps his covenant for a thousand generations and lavishes his unfailing love on those who love him and obey his commands."

Deuteronomy 7:9 nlt

A covenant is an agreement between two parties. Sure, we sign on the dotted line—or shake hands on a matter—but we don't always follow through. Not so with God. He always follows through on His agreement, even when we fall short. And He continues to lavish us with His unfailing love when we love Him back and obey His commands.

Disciplined by Love

The LORD disciplines those he loves,
as a father the son he delights in.

PROVERBS 3:12 NIV

When we discipline our children, it's because we love them and want the best for them. We're training them to be responsible adults. Same with God. He disciplines us out of love because He wants the very best for us. When we strike out on our own, away from His principles and blessings, He has no choice but to reel us back in. Love always disciplines.

Shaped by Love

*We are shaped and fashioned
by what we love.*

JOHANN WOLFGANG VON GOETHE

Likely you've heard the old expression
"You are what you eat!" We really do
"become" what we love, don't we? That's
why it's so important to love the Lord
our God with all of our hearts. We want
to become more like Him. When we love
Him, we're shaped and fashioned by His
words, His love, and His compassion for
humankind.

Tough Love

Accountability

*Love does not delight in evil
but rejoices with the truth.*

1 CORINTHIANS 13:6 NIV

It's so hard to watch someone you love get caught up in a sinful lifestyle– for instance, your teen is on drugs or your spouse turns to alcohol. For the first time, your love toward that person changes slightly. It toughens up. It gets a backbone. It says, "This far and no further." And it holds the other person accountable. Tough love. God's all for it. You will be, too, once you've seen its results.

God's Tough Love

"The LORD is slow to anger, abounding in love and forgiving sin and rebellion. Yet he does not leave the guilty unpunished; he punishes the children for the sin of the parents to the third and fourth generation."

NUMBERS 14:18 NIV

God is a loving heavenly Father, but He knows how to implement tough love when the situation calls for it. Take Adam and Eve, for instance. Was there ever a more obvious instance of tough love than kicking them out of the garden when they sinned? Yes, God is the author of love—sweet and tough. He believes in consequences. When the need arises, don't be afraid to follow God's example. Love tough.

Love Says No

"Anyone who loves their father or mother more than me is not worthy of me; anyone who loves their son or daughter more than me is not worthy of me."

MATTHEW 10:37 NIV

Sometimes love has to be tough. It has to say no. It has to set limits. If you've been the parent of a teen, you know what it feels like to implement tough love. It's uncomfortable at times and can be a little tricky. You want that other person to know you love him or her, but you have to stick to your guns. God designed love to be both sweet and tough.

The Paradox

I have found the paradox, that if you love until it hurts, there can be no more hurt, only more love.

MOTHER TERESA

Sometimes love is painful. We love a rebellious teen and he doesn't love us back. We love a spouse who turns his back on us. We love a parent, who is so wrapped up in his work that he can't see beyond it to realize we're crying out for love. Yes, loving others who don't respond can be very difficult—and the way we love them changes—but our love never wanes, even in the hardest of times.

The Receiving End

What does the Lord your God
ask of you but to fear [him]
to walk in obedience to him,
to love him, to serve [him] with
all your heart and with all your soul.

DEUTERONOMY 10:12 NIV

If you've hurt others, then perhaps you know what it feels like to be on the receiving end of some tough love. There are consequences to doing the wrong thing, and they often involve years of proving that you're trustworthy after letting someone down. Forgiveness and the rebuilding of trust take time. Receiving tough love is uncomfortable, but don't fight it. Let love win the battle. Relationships will be restored and hearts will be mended.

Love and Patience

Love Is Patient

*Love is patient, love is kind.
It does not envy, it does not boast,
it is not proud. It does not dishonor
others, it is not self-seeking, it is
not easily angered, it keeps no
record of wrongs.*

1 CORINTHIANS 13:4–5 NIV

Oh, how impatient we are! We want what
we want—and we want it now! No waiting.
But love isn't impatient. It doesn't demand
immediate service. Instead, love waits
patiently on the sidelines. The next time
you feel yourself losing your patience, take a
deep breath. Remind yourself: love holds on
for the ride.

Love's First Duty

The first duty of love is to listen.
PAUL TILLICH

We live in such a fast-paced world that it's hard to keep up! Somewhere between fast food, disposable diapers, and microwaves, we conclude that everything in life needs to move in a hurry. But love shouldn't be rushed. When you really love someone, you're patient with that person. Your first "love duty" is to listen. Simply listen.

Patience and Understanding

A patient man has great understanding, but one who is quick-tempered displays folly.

PROVERBS 14:29 NIV

Ever wonder why some people are more understanding than others? They're not quick-tempered. They take the time to think things through. That's how love is. It doesn't knee-jerk. Doesn't react quickly. Love responds with understanding and thoughtfulness, not foolish words or a sharp retort. Take a deep breath, my friend! Let love and patience rule the day!

Patience—a Fine Companion

Patience is the companion of wisdom.
AUGUSTINE

Patience is a wonderful companion of wisdom, and we could also say that patience is a fine companion of love as well. For when you love others, you're naturally patient with them. You let them think things through. You give them time to change when change is necessary. You don't rush them toward the goal. Patience and love—try them on for size today.

Joyful in Hope

Be joyful in hope, patient in affliction,
faithful in prayer.

ROMANS 12:12 NIV

Hope is a precious commodity, isn't it? When we're hopeful, we can endure almost anything. It gives us the ability to patiently endure even the toughest of challenges. And hope is also a wonderful companion to love. When you love people, you find yourself treating them with more patience. You're hopeful that the relationships God has blessed you with are going to grow stronger and stronger as time goes by.

Building Others Up

Built Up by Love

Love and faithfulness keep a king safe;
through love his throne is made secure.

PROVERBS 20:28 NIV

Did you know it takes a thousand "'Atta boys!" to overcome one critical word? It's human nature to hang on to the negative words. Criticism rings loud and clear in our ears, but not praise. That's why it's so important to build others up with your love. Speak positive, affirming words. Encourage. Uplift. Make the other person feel safe and secure around you. Love doesn't tear down. It builds up.

Only What Is Helpful

Do not let any unwholesome talk come out of your mouths, but only what is helpful for building others up according to their needs, that it may benefit those who listen.

EPHESIANS 4:29 NIV

Oh, how we love to talk about others. Usually we don't set out to gossip or cause pain, but often that's how things end up. We get carried away. We share our "concerns" with others. God longs for us to guard what we say, dwelling only on what is helpful. That's how love operates. It compels us to build others up, not cut them down. May every word be beneficial.

Love—the Perfect Sweetener

Life is the flower for which love is the honey.

VICTOR HUGO

According to the Bible, the power of life and death is in the tongue. Words can make or break us. We need to speak words of love while we have the time, especially with our children. Whether we're talking to our friends, spouse, or children, what comes out of our mouths is important. We have to think of love as we would a cube of sugar. It's the perfect sweetener.

Love. . .the Best Medicine

Love is the best medicine, and there is more than enough to go around once you open your heart.

JULIE MARIE

Perhaps you've heard it said that laughter is the best medicine. Truly, love is the best medicine. When administered properly—and at the right time—it can mean the difference between life and death. Think of the people the Lord has placed in your life, the ones who most need your words of life. Today why not administer the medicine they need? Open your heart and pour out love.

Spur One Another On

*And let us consider how we may
spur one another on toward love
and good deeds.*

HEBREWS 10:24 NIV

Do you have a friend who needs your
encouragement? One who needs a real
boost? Ask yourself, "How can I spur
her on? What can I say that will make a
difference?" Can you write her a note of
encouragement? Speak words of faith
regarding her situation? Love spurs us on,
and words of kindness from a friend do the
same. Take time to build up your friend in
love.

The Love Song

Delightful Love

Let him kiss me with the kisses of his mouth—for your love is more delightful than wine.

SONG OF SONGS 1:2 NIV

It's interesting to think of our relationship with God as an intimate love relationship, isn't it? Yet that is the image He uses to talk about how He cares for us and how we should care for Him. Perhaps that's because the intimacy between a husband and wife reflects genuine love on so many levels. The depth of caring is deeper than in any other relationship. Spend intimate time with the Lord today.

Leaping across Mountains

Listen! My beloved! Look! Here he comes, leaping across the mountains, bounding over the hills. My lover is like a gazelle or a young stag.

SONG OF SONGS 2:8–9 NIV

God desires that we enter into an intimate relationship with Him. He runs to us when we're at our lowest point, offering a shoulder to weep on and words of comfort. He longs for us to curl up in His lap and share our heartbreaks. And He celebrates with us when we're having a great day. We are His bride! He cares about everything that affects us. Why? Because He's madly in love with us!

We Belong to Each Other

My lover is mine, and I am his.
SONG OF SONGS 2:16 NLT

There's something very special about the relationship between an earthly husband and wife. When you're married, you can say, "We belong to each other!" and mean it. The same is true of the relationship between Christ and His bride, the church. We belong to Him, and He belongs to us! We're knit together. Bound by love. Woven together by grace.

Soul-Kissed

For it was not into my ear you whispered, but into my heart. It was not my lips you kissed, but my soul.

JUDY GARLAND

Isn't it amazing to think about being in relationship with the King of kings and Lord of lords? He loves us! He adores us in the same way a bridegroom adores his bride. That love protects, saves, and encourages. And the God of the universe takes the time to whisper sweet nothings in our ears. He speaks words of life and encouragement. What a loving groom!

179

A Seal over Your Heart

Place me like a seal over your heart, like a seal on your arm; for love is as strong as death, its jealousy unyielding as the grave. It burns like blazing fire, like a mighty flame.

SONG OF SONGS 8:6 NIV

Love has placed its seal on our hearts. It says, "This one is mine! Don't touch!" God is jealous for us. He doesn't want us giving pieces of our hearts to the world. He longs for us to be a faithful bride in every respect. If you've wandered away from your Bridegroom, return to Him today. Let the flame of His love burn in your heart and restore you fully.

Satisfied by Love

A Satisfied Soul

Because your love is better than life,
my lips will glorify you. I will be fully
satisfied as with the richest of foods;
with singing lips my mouth will praise you.

PSALM 63:3–5 NIV

Ah, satisfaction! Such a comforting
feeling. Did you know that God wants us to
be satisfied with His love? Our souls can be
satisfied in Him. So what does it mean to be
satisfied? It means we're okay with His plan,
not ours. We trust in His love for us. He has
our best interests at heart. Today allow the
Lord's overwhelming love to satisfy your
heart, your mind, and your soul.

Be Glad!

Satisfy us in the morning with your unfailing love, that we may sing for joy and be glad all our days.

PSALM 90:14 NIV

Can you imagine waking up satisfied every morning? God's unfailing love can cause you to do that. You can wake up with a song on your lips and a happy heart. Why? Because His love sustains you through the night. It gets you through the dark places. The valleys. You awake to a new day, fresh with His love and His insight. Ah, morning! What a wonderful time to praise!

Making Up for the Lack

If you have love in your life, it can make up for a great many things you lack. If you don't have it, no matter what else there is. . .it's not enough.

ANN LANDERS

Oh, how we long for "stuff." We want what everyone else has—a nice car, a roomy house, sharp clothes, and a great paying job. We're rarely satisfied with what we have. God's love can satisfy us and squelch the never-ending desire for more stuff. Sure, it's fine to have things—as long as they don't have us. God's love—and the love of our family and friends—really does make up for the lack of material possessions.

Joyful Are Those

*Praise the LORD! How joyful are
those who fear the LORD and
delight in obeying his commands.
Their children will be successful
everywhere; an entire generation
of godly people will be blessed.*

PSALM 112:1–2 NLT

When we're fully aware of God's love for us—and for our children—we can be more than satisfied. We can be joyful! Why? Because He has us covered. He sees our needs and meets them. He loves us with an everlasting love. And His blessings aren't just for us; they're for an entire generation of godly people! Talk about a reason to celebrate!

With Long Life

*"With a long life I will satisfy him
and let him see My salvation."*

PSALM 91:16 NASB

Have you ever seen the look of contentment in the face of an older believer? Next time you're around someone in his golden years, take time to examine his expression. What you will find is contentment. Satisfaction. He's walked with God a long time and knows that the Lord won't leave or forsake him. He has seen God's salvation in this lifetime and looks forward to heaven, which is right around the bend.

Unfailing Love

Under the Shadow

How precious is your unfailing love,
O God! All humanity finds shelter in
the shadow of your wings.

PSALM 36:7 NLT

People fail us. They say they're going to do something, and then they don't. They promise to stick with us, and then they leave. We even fail others, making promises we don't keep. But God isn't a failure, and neither is His love. We can trust in His unfailing love. In fact, we can live under its shadow all the days of our lives!

Trust in His Love

But I trust in your unfailing love;
my heart rejoices in your salvation.

PSALM 13:5 NIV

Some of us have trust issues, don't we?
We've been let down so many times, we have
trouble trusting anyone, even God. Here's
the good news: God is trustworthy! He won't
let you down. Won't leave you hanging.
We can trust in His unfailing love, and we
can trust that He's going to do what He has
promised.

Love as You Say You Love

Many claim to have unfailing love,
but a faithful person who can find?
PROVERBS 20:6 NIV

I love yous" are a dime a dozen. We hear them on TV, read them in books, and see them in gossip magazines. Everyone is in love, but usually not for long. Though they say the words, many would-be lovers change their minds after a short time. If you're looking for a "forever" kind of love, look to God. He loves as He says He loves, and He can teach you to do the same!

Silenced by Love

In your unfailing love,
silence my enemies; destroy
all my foes, for I am your servant.

PSALM 143:12 NIV

God's unfailing love is powerful. It can cause us to rise up and shout for joy, and it can silence our enemies in a second. When we follow after the Lord, His love comes with a "protective" feature: it stops our enemies in their tracks. Oh, it might not happen right away, but love eventually wins out!

Unshaken—and Unfailing

"Though the mountains be shaken and the hills be removed, yet my unfailing love for you will not be shaken nor my covenant of peace be removed," says the LORD, who has compassion on you.

ISAIAH 54:10 NIV

Life doesn't always go the way we hope it does. We face storms. Challenges. We're wounded by people we love, and we feel like curling up in a ball and forgetting about life. God's unfailing love woos us from our place of pain and reminds us that the shaking won't last forever. His covenant of peace lasts forever. We really can be unshaken, as long as we abide in His unfailing love.

Love—with All Your Heart

With All Your Heart

Jesus said to him, " 'You shall love the LORD your God with all your heart, with all your soul, and with all your mind.' This is the first and great commandment. And the second is like it: 'You shall love your neighbor as yourself.' On these two commandments hang all the Law and the Prophets."

MATTHEW 22:37–40 NKJV

Jesus commands us to do two things: Love God and love others. That seems so simple, yet it's so hard! If we truly loved God with all of our hearts—laying down our own wants, wishes, and desires—it would revolutionize our lives! Here's the great part: It's possible to live like this! Love God. Love people. Watch as God transforms your world!

191

A Priceless Gift

Love is a symbol of eternity. It wipes out all sense of time, destroying all memory of a beginning and all fear of an end.

AUTHOR UNKNOWN

God's love is everlasting and unfailing. Best of all, it's poured out freely from the hands of a merciful God who longs for us to love others with the same passion, the same zeal. When we're wrapped up in love, time seems to stand still. All that matters is right here right now. Fear is banished. Sins are forgiven. We stand washed, cleaned—loved. What a priceless, eternal gift!

Joined Together

*Speaking the truth in love,
we will grow to become in every
respect the mature body of him who
is the Head, that is, Christ. From him
the whole body, joined and held together
by every supporting ligament, grows
and builds itself up in love,
as each part does its work.*

EPHESIANS 4:15–16 NIV

Love graces us through our mistakes and joins us together as one body, the bride of Christ. We learn how to love by reading the Bible and spending time with God, who gave us the ultimate example of "how to" love when He sent His Son to die in our place. All He asks in return is that we give our hearts to Him. Go forth and love, dear friends!

Loving People for Who They Are

Looking at the Heart

"People look at the outward appearance, but the Lord looks at the heart."

1 SAMUEL 16:7 NIV

We tend to judge people by outward appearance, and sometimes the way we treat them is affected as well. Thankfully, God loves us despite our spots and wrinkles! And He calls us to love others in spite of any physical flaws. If you want to show the love of God to friends or coworkers, don't judge them by what they wear, their hairstyles, or their choice of makeup (or lack thereof). Just love them. Period.

Loving in Spite
of Differences

*But when the kindness and love of God
our Savior appeared, he saved us, not
because of righteous things we had
done, but because of his mercy.*

TITUS 3:4–5 NIV

We're all different. All unique. God created
us as individuals on purpose! We have
different philosophies, different political
views, and different ways of communicating.
Thankfully, God's love supersedes all of
these differences. We are called to love in
spite of them. Today, instead of getting
riled up at an acquaintance who sees things
differently than you do, extend love. It
covers a multitude of differences.

Five Minutes

If we discovered that we had only five minutes left to say all that we wanted to say, every telephone booth would be occupied by people calling other people to stammer that they loved them.

CHRISTOPHER MORLEY

Have you ever thought about what your final words will be to those you love? Most likely you won't be offering critique or telling people what they need to change. No, it's far more likely you will be fighting to get one final "I love you" out for all to hear. Those words are really all that matter in the end, aren't they?

Worship Styles

For in Christ Jesus neither circumcision
nor uncircumcision counts for anything,
but only faith working through love.
GALATIANS 5:6 ESV

The body of Christ is made up of millions
of people around the globe. We're like
snowflakes. No two of us are alike. Sure,
we praise the same God, but we worship
differently. Some praise with great
enthusiasm. Others prefer a quiet, peaceful
worship service. Instead of focusing on our
differences, love sees past them and strives
for unity. What is the one thing that unites
us? Jesus! And Jesus is love.

Problem-Solving Love

*Never let a problem to be
solved become more important
than a person to be loved.*

BARBARA JOHNSON

So often we set out to offer advice, hoping
to change people. We say we're doing it
for their own good, but oftentimes we're
really just trying to shape them into our
image. Love doesn't seek to change people.
Only God can bring change. So if the
person you're trying to "adjust" doesn't
seem to want to budge, don't consider it
problematic. Love the person. Let God do
the rest.

Everlasting Love

From Everlasting to Everlasting

But from everlasting to everlasting the LORD's love is with those who fear him, and his righteousness with their children's children.

PSALM 103:17 NIV

Isn't it interesting to think that God has existed forever? Before He created the heavens and the earth, He was. And He will be here in the "forever" yet to come, as well. Even more amazing, God has been in love with His people forever. He loved humankind in the garden, and He will love us long after we're all in heaven with Him. His love truly reaches from everlasting to everlasting.

Drawn with
Loving-Kindness

"I have loved you with an everlasting love; I have drawn you with unfailing kindness."

JEREMIAH 31:3 NIV

Infinity is a difficult concept to grasp. When we say the word *forever*, we're keenly aware that the forever life goes far beyond what we experience here on earth. When we ask Jesus to come into our hearts and He becomes Lord of our lives, we step into a "forever" existence with Him. And His love lasts forever, too. It's not just meant for the here and now, but for all eternity. Praise God for His everlasting love!

Flourishing in God's Love

But I am like an olive tree flourishing in the house of God; I trust in God's unfailing love for ever and ever.

PSALM 52:8 NIV

When we trust in God's unfailing, everlasting love, we flourish like trees planted by streams of living water. We continue to grow and thrive. As you ponder this "forever" love that God offers through His Son, trust that He will walk you through the rest of your days stronger than you've ever been. You can flourish in God's everlasting love!

I Hope in Him

The Lord's love never ends;
his mercies never stop.
They are new every morning;
LORD, your loyalty is great. I say
to myself, "The LORD is mine,
so I hope in him."

LAMENTATIONS 3:22–24 NCV

God's love is steadfast. Steady. Unwavering. It isn't tossed about by every wind, blown here and there. When we love others, our feelings sometimes shift. We're hot one day, cold the next. Not so with the Lord. He's in it for the long haul, even when we mess up. And this steadfast love keeps us through this life and the life to come. All praise to the One whose mercies never come to an end!

Glory Forever and Ever

*To him who loves us and has freed us
from our sins by his blood, and has made
us to be a kingdom and priests to serve
his God and Father—to him be glory
and power for ever and ever! Amen.*

REVELATION 1:5–6 NIV

Oh, how the love of God propels us to praise! His everlasting love has saved us, freed us, and made us His heirs, His children, His own. There's no other place we can go to receive such unconditional love. May we continue to worship Him from now until eternity, offering praise and glory for this spectacular love!

Scripture Index

Old Testament

New Testament

Notes

Notes

Notes